LIVING
IN THE
GLORY
EVERY DAY

OTHER BOOKS BY DAVID HERZOG

AVAILABLE FROM DESTINY IMAGE PUBLISHERS

LIVING
IN THE
GLORY
EVERY DAY

DAVID HERZOG

Compiled by Jan Sherman

DESTINY IMAGE® PUBLISHERS, INC.
P.O. Box 310, Shippensburg, PA 17257-0310

"Speaking to the Purposes of God for This Generation and for the Generations to Come."

This book and all other Destiny Image, Revival Press, MercyPlace, Fresh Bread, Destiny Image Fiction, and Treasure House books are available at Christian bookstores and distributors worldwide.

For a U.S. bookstore nearest you, call 1-800-722-6774.
For more information on foreign distributors, call 717-532-3040.
Reach us on the Internet: www.destinyimage.com.

ISBN 10: 0-7684-3160-3   ISBN 13: 978-0-7684-3160-5

For Worldwide Distribution, Printed in the U.S.A.
1 2 3 4 5 6 7 8 9 10 11 / 13 12 11 10

CONTENTS

DAY 1

THE SPIRIT OF ELIJAH

*Behold, I am going to send you Elijah the prophet
before the coming of the great and terrible day
of the Lord* (Malachi 4:5 NASB).

DEVOTION FOR TODAY

We are seeing the restoration of the spirit of Elijah upon the Church. In this new move of God, there is not only an increase in signs and wonders, but there are also unusual and creative miracles (including resurrections from the dead), angelic visitations, and the restoration of key revelations, mysteries, and truths that have been lost through the centuries. Some of the things we are experiencing are familiar, but many things are brand-new—another wave of greater glory. It has been more than 50 years now since the last great miracle revival took place and 50 years since Israel became a nation. God ordained that Jubilee, the restoration of all that has been lost, occur every 50 years. This is the time of restoration.

SOMETHING TO THINK ABOUT

1. Why do you think Elijah is used as the prophet that exemplifies the revival of the Church before the Lord's return?

_____

_____

_____

2. Have you personally seen an increase in signs and wonders in the Church? Why or why not?

_____

_____

_____

3. From what you understand, how does the principle of the year of Jubilee lend itself to the Church's current position to experience revival?

_____

_____

_____

MEDITATION

"We need *the knowledge of the glory of the Lord*" (Hab. 2:14) to see the heavens opened and the mysteries of the glory unveiled! (*Mysteries of the Glory Unveiled,* p. 19). In what way do you need the knowledge of the Lord's glory?

_____

_____

_____

_____

_____

_____

_____

_____

DAY 2

A REVIVAL OF SIGNS AND WONDERS

...tell John...that the blind see, the lame walk, the lepers are cleansed, the deaf hear, the dead are raised, the poor have the gospel preached to them... (Luke 7:22-23).

DEVOTION FOR TODAY

God seems to package revival in such a way as to attract only those who are desperate for Him. The hungry are somehow able to see what God is doing through strange new circumstances, rather than judging by outward appearances. When people are expecting God to bring revival in the way they have known in the past but it actually comes in a totally different form, it seems easy for them to reject it. It is sad that they keep waiting for something else to come along when something new is already happening. In the days ahead we will see many of the same miracles that accompanied Jesus, and these signs and wonders will also be too many and too diverse to be recorded.

SOMETHING TO THINK ABOUT

1. Why do you think Jesus told John's disciples to tell him about the signs and wonders that accompanied His powerful preaching?

_____

_____

_____

2. In your opinion, why do many people reject the ways in which God moves? Have you ever been skeptical of a "demonstration of power" that seemed suspect?

_____

_____

_____

3. Do you think there are any restrictions as to what means God can use to demonstrate His authority and power?

_____

_____

_____

MEDITATION

"The revival of signs and wonders is the most powerful and biblical way to witness to Jews and Muslims, those in the occult, New Age, false religions, atheists and most of the unreached people groups in the world today. After all, this is the way Jesus did it" (*Mysteries of the Glory Unveiled*, p. 36). Why do you think this is true?

_____

_____

_____

_____

_____

_____

_____

_____

Day 3

A Harvest-producing Rain

Ask the Lord for rain in the time of the latter rain. The Lord will make flashing clouds; He will give them showers of rain… (Zechariah 10:1).

Devotion for Today

Most of us who are attuned to God's Spirit have come to believe that a great harvest of souls is on His immediate agenda. Throughout history, great outpourings of the Holy Spirit have been accompanied by a great harvest of souls. The first such outpouring took place, of course, on the Day of Pentecost. That day, people were refreshed, revived, empowered, and filled with joy. Soon thereafter, 3,000 souls were saved, and this great harvest of souls continued in the fledgling Church on a daily basis. As the harvest grew ever larger, people in the affected areas became alarmed and persecution broke out against the Church. Consequently, the disciples needed another wave of empowerment so they could remain faithful to God.

SOMETHING TO THINK ABOUT

1. In your experience, why does a great outpouring of God's Spirit produce a great harvest of souls?

   _____

   _____

   _____

2. What kinds of stress do you think the New Testament Church experienced as it increased in size so rapidly?

   _____

   _____

   _____

3. How might it be easy to begin to do things in the flesh rather than ask for another wave of outpouring when such an overwhelming number of souls were saved?

   _____

   _____

   _____

MEDITATION

"And when they had prayed…and they were all filled with the Holy Spirit, and they spoke the Word of God with boldness" (Acts 4:31). In your experience, how are the Holy Spirit and boldness related?

_____

_____

_____

_____

_____

_____

_____

_____

DAY 4

THE HARVEST IS MULTIPLIED

Then the churches…were edified. And walking in the fear of the Lord and in the comfort of the Holy Spirit, they were multiplied (Acts 9:31).

DEVOTION FOR TODAY

Each time the Holy Spirit is poured out over a thirsty land, it produces a harvest. Each wave of outpouring brought with it a wave of harvest, each increase in the power of God bringing an increase in the number of souls saved. The Azusa Street Revival of the early years of the twentieth century was an outpouring of the Holy Spirit that brought with it a new surge of power and the baptism of the Holy Spirit. This led to great harvest around the world. Statistics reveal that by 1990, more than 372 million people had been affected by this outpouring. The Azusa Street Revival is Mysteries of the Glory Unveiled, the foundation on which the Pentecostal and Charismatic movements stand.

SOMETHING TO THINK ABOUT

1. What do you think it means in Acts 9:31 when it says that the churches were *"edified"*? How did this edification prepare them for multiplication?

_____

_____

_____

2. What do you think it takes to make Christians thirsty enough to produce a harvest? What do Christians need to be thirsty for?

_____

_____

_____

3. How does the power of God spread beyond the meetings and worship services where it is experienced?

_____

_____

_____

MEDITATION

"...And the Lord added to the church daily those who were being saved" (Acts 2:47). How might we experience a daily increase to the Church when we meet only a few times a week or is meeting more often corporately what this is really referring to?

_____

_____

_____

_____

_____

_____

_____

_____

DAY 5

THE GRAIN HAS RIPENED

*Then He will continue to send both the early
and late rains that will produce wonderful
crops of grain* (Deuteronomy 11:14 TLB).

DEVOTION FOR TODAY

Gold is the color of harvest. Wheat, especially when it is ready to collect, has a beautiful golden color. As God pours out His Spirit in this unusual way, the golden glory is attracting people in record numbers. This has proven to be a most powerful tool for evangelism. People are curious, and this manifestation draws the curious. But there are other reasons. The gold is a visible sign that the glory of God has returned to His people, and that glory draws men and women. Men who have *"sinned and come short of the glory of God"* (Rom. 3:23) are drawn to it when they hear that it has appeared. When they see gold manifested, they are drawn to repentance and are saved.

SOMETHING TO THINK ABOUT

1. What do you think marks the early and late rains (see Scripture on page 23) in terms of the harvest of souls for the Kingdom of God?

   _____

   _____

   _____

2. Why do you think curiosity helps bring people to see God's unusual manifestations of power?

   _____

   _____

   _____

3. What do you see as the correlation between the appearance of gold and the glory of God?

   _____

   _____

   _____

MEDITATION

"The Gentiles shall come to your light, And kings to the brightness of your rising..." (Isa. 60:3). Why is it that when the glory of God is seen upon us, people are attracted to it?

_____

_____

_____

_____

_____

_____

_____

Day 6

The First Fruits of Our Prayers

…the seventh time…he said, "There is a cloud, as small as a man's hand, rising out of the sea! …go down before the rain stops you" (1 Kings 18:44).

Devotion for Today

Some are still looking for the return of a former revival, like Elijah's servant who went out and looked seven times and saw nothing promising. But we have already reaped the first fruits of our prayers. Miracle revival is coming, for the sign of it, the first drops of golden rain, have appeared. If you have looked seven times and haven't seen anything promising, look again. A cloud "as small as a man's hand" probably did not impress Elijah's servant, but it excited Elijah because he knew what it represented. The golden rain we are experiencing is often in very tiny droplets. It is not even as large as a man's hand, but we know what it represents. Good things are on the way.

SOMETHING TO THINK ABOUT

1. In your opinion, why do many of us expect God to act and demonstrate Who He is in the same ways as we have seen in the past?

_____

_____

_____

2. Do you find it easy or difficult to believe God when He shows Himself in very small ways? Why or why not?

_____

_____

_____

3. How can you find personal encouragement about what God is going to do in the future based on the small pockets of miracles that are taking place today?

_____

_____

_____

Meditation

"Respond to the signs God is sending and rejoice in them, no matter how insignificant you might consider them to be" (*Mysteries of the Glory Unveiled,* p. 49). Why do we need to act on minimal assurance, just as Elijah's servant did?

_____

_____

_____

_____

_____

_____

_____

DAY 7

THE KEY TO CREATIVE MIRACLES

In the beginning…the earth was formless…and darkness covered the deep waters. And the Spirit of God was hovering over the surface… God said, "Let there be light…" (Genesis 1:1-3 NLT).

DEVOTION FOR TODAY

When the presence of God, His glory, begins to hover over a place or a person, the power and potential for creative miracles is present. It is an act so simple that most of us miss it. When the presence of God is hovering over you in a given place and you hear His voice, learn to obey spontaneously as He is saying it, and when you do, creative miracles will begin to manifest themselves. Even though we sense that the glory of God is hovering over us, it is easy to let our reasoning get in the way of action. We use our faith to tap into God's glory, but once we do, acting creatively demands only that we listen and obey.

SOMETHING TO THINK ABOUT

1. How do you recognize when the presence of God and His glory hover over a person or place? Why is this easy to miss?

_____

_____

_____

2. Is it easy for you to be spontaneous in your obedience, or do you find spontaneity disconcerting? Why or why not?

_____

_____

_____

3. How does your reasoning talk you out of acting on God's voice? Where does your faith need to tap in so that obedience becomes your only response?

_____

_____

_____

MEDITATION

"The quicker we act on what God is saying, the more easily and dramatically the creative miracle will occur" (*Mysteries of the Glory Unveiled,* p. 55). Think about what this statement means and explain how this principle works.

_____

_____

_____

_____

_____

_____

_____

_____

DAY 8

GOING BEYOND THE LIMITS
OF OUR OWN FAITH

*But you do not believe, because you are not
of My sheep…My sheep hear My voice, and I
know them, and they follow Me* (John 10:26-27).

DEVOTION FOR TODAY

When we become convinced that the Creator Himself is speaking through us, we know that all we must do is obey. We use our faith to tap into God's glory, but once we do, acting creatively demands that we only listen and obey. The work to be done is a work of the Creator. It is His glory that does the work, not anything that we can do ourselves. When we learn to speak before we have had the chance to analyze the impossibility of what we are saying, the miracle is already done. Entering the creative realm is as simple as hearing the Lord and following His instructions.

The power of God's spoken word is awesome. It is eternal. It is creative.

SOMETHING TO THINK ABOUT

1. What does it take to convince you that the Creator Himself is speaking through you? Does He speak the same way each time?

_____

_____

_____

2. How do you use your faith to tap into God's glory? How does His glory demand that we only listen and obey?

_____

_____

_____

3. Explain how a miracle is already done when we speak what God says before we have analyzed its impossibility.

_____

_____

_____

MEDITATION

"After God spoke the planets and galaxies into existence, His word did not become powerless. He is still capable of creation, and when we believe Him, He still creates" (*Mysteries of the Glory Unveiled*, p. 56). What does this mean to you personally?

_____

_____

_____

_____

_____

_____

_____

_____

Day 9

Future or Present Tense?

For we are His workmanship, created in Christ Jesus for good works, which God prepared beforehand that we should walk in them (Ephesians 2:10).

Devotion for Today

Usually we think of prophetic words as being in the future tense. We need to change that mind-set. Whether a word is in future tense or present tense depends on us. Once it is spoken, it is there to be walked into. "*For I am ready to set things right, **not in the distant future, but right now!***" (Isa. 46:13 NLT). What has God promised to you? Whatever it is, it already exists. It was created when He spoke it. It is no longer a question of when the promise of God will come to pass. The question now is: *When will you start walking into it?* Once you have the understanding that it already exists, you have faith to walk into it.

SOMETHING TO THINK ABOUT

1. Have you usually thought of prophetic words as
   being in the future tense? Why do you think this
   is easy for us to think in this way?

   _____

   _____

   _____

2. In what way does Isaiah 46:13 show you God's
   perspective of time and His creative works?

   _____

   _____

   _____

3. What do you need in order to walk in God's
   promises and make the future become your pres-
   ent-day life?

   _____

   _____

   _____

MEDITATION

"The Word of God tells us that Jesus is *'the Lamb slain from the foundation of the world'* (Rev. 13:8)" (*Mysteries of the Glory Unveiled,* p. 64). How does this example speak to what God has prepared for your life right now?

_____

_____

_____

_____

_____

_____

_____

_____

Day 10

A New Outpouring of Power

And when they had prayed, the place where they were assembled together was shaken; and they were all filled with the Holy Spirit... (Acts 4:31).

Devotion for Today

Each new move of the Spirit has a new outpouring of power that comes with it and new manifestations and new truths that are revealed. We go "from glory to glory," and each new glory has a new manifestation. If the apostles had insisted that the experience of the initial Day of Pentecost outpouring was the only pattern for revival, they never would have progressed. When a move of God's Spirit stops moving, it is no longer a move, and it becomes part of history. When God moves in a new way, we cannot always compare it to past moves to see if it is of Him. If we are to be pioneers, we must allow God to do things that bypass our current experience.

SOMETHING TO THINK ABOUT

1. What are the differences that you see in the apostles' experience in Acts 2 and the one they experienced in Acts 4?

   _____

   _____

   _____

2. What do you think going "from glory to glory" means to the Church? What does this mean to you personally?

   _____

   _____

   _____

3. What do you think it takes to allow God to bypass your current experience with Him? Do you think most Christians would answer the same as you?

   _____

   _____

   _____

MEDITATION

"What we seek is usually what we find, especially if we are seeking after what God has promised us" (*Mysteries of the Glory Unveiled,* p. 76). For what are you currently seeking? Are you desperate for what you are seeking?

_____

_____

_____

_____

_____

_____

_____

_____

DAY 11

A REVIVAL OF WISDOM

For the earth will be filled with the knowledge of the glory of the Lord, as the waters cover the sea (Habakkuk 2:14).

DEVOTION FOR TODAY

Often we say that the earth will be filled with the glory of the Lord, rather than with the *knowledge* of the glory of the Lord. When we have the knowledge, we not only sense the glory, but we have the key to releasing miracles and manifestations from that glory. Some wonder why they have sensed the glory, without ever seeing a physical manifestation of that glory. Having the knowledge of the glory makes the difference.

The glory could be likened to a cloud. The people see the cloud, but they lack the knowledge or wisdom necessary to make it rain. Clouds come and go sometimes without yielding rain. Now God is revealing the keys to releasing spiritual rain from the clouds of glory.

SOMETHING TO THINK ABOUT

1. What is the difference between the earth being filled with the glory of the Lord and the earth being filled with the knowledge of the glory of the Lord?

_____

_____

_____

2. In your experience, have you often sensed God's glory without seeing any physical manifestations of his glory?

_____

_____

_____

3. How should we pursue the knowledge of God's glory? What wisdom is necessary to "make it rain"?

_____

_____

_____

Meditation

"...the eyes of your understanding being enlightened; that you may know what is the hope of His calling..." (Eph. 1:18). How does the revelation of your calling give you knowledge and wisdom to access His glory?

_____

_____

_____

_____

_____

_____

_____

_____

DAY 12

ANGELIC VISITATIONS

Then he dreamed… a ladder was set up on the earth, and…reached to Heaven; and…angels… were ascending and descending… (Genesis 28:12).

DEVOTION FOR TODAY

Another of the miraculous aspects of this new move of God's glory is that we are beginning to see much more angelic activity. God is opening the heavens to His people. He is taking us into the heavens, and He is bringing the heavens down to us. Just as it has been said that the enemy, knowing that his time is short, is unleashing multitudes of demons upon the earth, so God is releasing more angels to help us in this end-time harvest. More and more believers are speaking about being taken to Heaven in the spirit and returning. Others are seeing angels in their churches and in their homes. Some are seeing the Lord Jesus Himself. The gap between Heaven and earth is being bridged.

SOMETHING TO THINK ABOUT

1. Have you had experience with angelic activity or know someone who has? What effects has angelic activity had on the Church?

   _____

   _____

   _____

2. Why do you think God is taking more believers into Heaven and returning them to earth? What purpose might this have?

   _____

   _____

   _____

3. What do you think it means when the author says, "The gap between Heaven and earth is being bridged"? Bridged by what means?

   _____

   _____

   _____

DAY 12

MEDITATION

"Jesus taught us to pray, 'Thy will be done on earth as it is in Heaven'—this is becoming possible in the glory" (*Mysteries of the Glory Unveiled*, p. 128). Think about what this possibility will mean to you personally.

_____

_____

_____

_____

_____

_____

_____

_____

DAY 13

TRANSPORTED IN THE SPIRIT

*The hand of the Lord came upon me and
brought me out in the Spirit of the Lord, and
set me down in the midst of the valley; and
it was full of bones* (Ezekiel 37:1).

DEVOTION FOR TODAY

Ezekiel was transported in the Spirit. In the days
ahead, as we become more and more acquainted
with this realm of glory, we will come to realize
just how unlimited it is. Distance is nothing in the glory,
and God can easily transport us from place to place.

The apostle Paul carried many concerns for the
young churches throughout the Roman Empire, but
because he traveled so much, it was sometimes
impossible for him to be physically present to deal
with some of their problems.

This did not seem to limit him. He wrote:

*For though I am absent in the flesh, yet I am with
you in spirit, rejoicing to see your good order and
the steadfastness of your faith in Christ* (Colos-
sians 2:5).

SOMETHING TO THINK ABOUT

1. Can you imagine God transporting you in the Spirit to another location to do His will? What are some of the purposes for which God may transport you?

_____

_____

_____

2. How is it possible that Paul was "absent in the flesh" (meaning that his body was not there) and still he rejoiced "to see [their] good order and the steadfastness of [their] faith in Christ"?

_____

_____

_____

3. Do you believe that Paul meant he was literally absent and that he was taken in the Spirit to them?

_____

_____

_____

Meditation

"For I indeed, as absent in body but present in spirit...when you are gathered together, along with my spirit..." (1 Cor. 5:3-5). How might you need to prepare to allow the Lord to transport you?

_____

_____

_____

_____

_____

_____

_____

_____

DAY 14

*So I prophesied as I was commanded; and as
I prophesied, there was a noise...and the bones
came together, bone to bone* (Ezekiel 37:7).

DEVOTION FOR TODAY

Through the revival of God's glory, He is
bringing a unity to the Body of Christ that is
miraculous. Just as the glory draws souls to
the light, it also brings together believers who seek
the same glory and the same harvest. Many groups
that have been separated throughout the years
(because of some doctrinal difference or emphasis)
are finding themselves unified in meetings where the
glory is manifested. This unity is important to continued revival. Many groups of Christians have been
seeking revival, but they are like the bones in the valley of Ezekiel's vision. They are completely separated
from one another. Before God can resurrect the dry
bones, He must first bring them together to form the
essential elements of the Body.

59

SOMETHING TO THINK ABOUT

1. Have you personally experienced a unity with believers who go to different churches or different streams or denominations? Why is this unity important?

   _____

   _____

   _____

2. How does God's manifested glory come as a result of the unity of purpose of different groups of people?

   _____

   _____

   _____

3. Why do those who seek revival often find themselves unable to see God's manifested glory?

   _____

   _____

   _____

MEDITATION

"The bones in Ezekiel's vision came together when Ezekiel prophesied, and as we declare and prophesy into existence this new move of God, something wonderful is happening behind the scenes" (*Mysteries of the Glory Unveiled,* p. 156). Meditate on what might be happening.

_____

_____

_____

_____

_____

_____

_____

DAY 15

THE PARTS OF THE ENGINE WORK TOGETHER

From whom the whole body, joined and knit together by what every joint supplies, according to the effective working by which every part does its share… (Ephesians 4:16).

DEVOTION FOR TODAY

For the Body of Christ to walk in full power and glory, all the parts must be in place and working together like a car's engine. If some elements of the engine are not well connected, it cannot even start, let alone run. This is also true of the Body of Christ. God is bringing the pieces together, for each of us has something so vital to the welfare of the whole that its absence can often make the difference between victory and defeat. When every part does its share, the fullness of God's glory will come, causing a major growth in the harvest. The more we are joined to the glory of God, the more we will find our places and function together.

63

SOMETHING TO THINK ABOUT

1. Are you joined and knitted together with your brothers and sisters in God's glory? Why or why not? What does this mean to your effectiveness?

_____

_____

_____

2. Are you aware that "every joint supplies" something to the Body? What is it that you supply to the Body of Christ?

_____

_____

_____

3. Why is it true that the more we are joined to God's glory, the more we will find our places and function together?

_____

_____

_____

MEDITATION

"Apart from the glory, our activities can be little more than manmade programs and ideas of unity. Unity is a miracle that only the Spirit can do for us but with our cooperation" *Mysteries of the Glory Unveiled,* (p. 167). Why is this true?

_____

_____

_____

_____

_____

_____

_____

_____

DAY 16

A RETURN TO OUR ROOTS

Then He said to me, "Son of man, these bones
are the whole house of Israel...I will...bring
you into the land of Israel" (Ezekiel 37:11-12).

DEVOTION FOR TODAY

There is much being talked about concerning unity and reconciliation among the various denominations, movements, and races in the Church. Most believers have yet to taste the power of the early Church. Greater things are prepared for us than for the early Church, because the latter will be greater than the former since God has promised to bring us the former and the latter rain together. As we venture into the new, however, we cannot forget where we came from. We must rediscover our roots and their power, and we would do well to examine closely what caused the power of the early Church to dwindle. This is important if we are to possess the fullness of what has been reserved for this generation.

SOMETHING TO THINK ABOUT

1. When we have true unity and reconciliation, what do you think will be the marks of our life together as the Church?

   _____

   _____

   _____

2. Why is it important to remember our spiritual heritage? Why do our roots help us to possess the fullness of God's power and glory?

   _____

   _____

   _____

3. Why do you think the early Church's power dwindled? Are there ways we need to be watchful in order to keep from making the same mistake?

   _____

   _____

   _____

MEDITATION

"Ezekiel prophesied to the dry bones, which were the whole house of Israel" (*Mysteries of the Glory Unveiled*, p. 171). What do you think the "whole house of Israel" means?

_____

_____

_____

_____

_____

_____

_____

DAY 17

THE CALL TO FORM
THE ONE NEW MAN

...The Deliverer will come out of Zion, And He will turn away ungodliness from Jacob; For this is My covenant with them... (Romans 11:26-27).

DEVOTION FOR TODAY

In this current move of God, a call is going forth to again form the One New Man. In the Messiah, this Body is to be made up of both Jew and Gentile believers. Will we heed the call and reconnect to our spiritual roots? If we are willing to do so, we will experience, in the days just ahead, a new surge of the power of God and will see the greatest harvest ever recorded. Already Jews are being drawn to the Messiah in record numbers. Destiny is knocking at the door. We must heed the call to support the preaching of the Gospel "to the Jew first." God has promised that in the last days there would be revival in modern-day Israel.

SOMETHING TO THINK ABOUT

1. Why do you think God is calling to form the One New Man in the Body of Messiah with both Jews and Gentiles? What is His purpose for doing this?

   _____

   _____

   _____

2. Why is it important to increase our connection to our spiritual roots (the Jewish people)? What will this connection open up for us?

   _____

   _____

   _____

3. Why should we preach the Gospel to the Jewish people first? What does this fulfill in the prophecies that speak about the last days?

   _____

   _____

   _____

MEDITATION

"We need a revelation of Israel and the Church to understand the importance of our union with every believer for the last-day harvest" (*Mysteries of the Glory Unveiled*, p. 185). Do you have this revelation of Israel and the Church?

_____

_____

_____

_____

_____

_____

_____

_____

DAY 18

THE ANCIENT PORTALS OF HEAVEN

*Stand in the ways and see, and ask
for the old paths, where the good way is,
and walk in it...* (Jeremiah 6:16).

DEVOTION FOR TODAY

There are ancient paths that open up ancient portals into the fullness of the supernatural and the glory of God. Great men of old like Enoch, Moses, Elijah, Adam, Paul, Jesus, and others walked in these ancient paths. What did these Jewish prophets and apostles know so that they could call down fire from Heaven, command rain, or shut up the sky? There is a parallel world of the supernatural living side by side with this natural realm. Once we tap into the supernatural realm and the revelation of these ancient paths, we will realize it is just a hand's length away as you reach out for it: *"The Kingdom of Heaven is at hand"* (Matt. 4:17).

SOMETHING TO THINK ABOUT

1. What are some of the ways the following people were able to move in the fullness of the supernatural: Moses, Daniel, Enoch, Paul, Jesus?

   _____

   _____

   _____

2. What do you think these great men knew that we have lost today? Use Jeremiah 6:16 to postulate your answer.

   _____

   _____

   _____

3. Describe what you know about the supernatural realm and how it parallels the natural realm.

   _____

   _____

   _____

DAY 18

MEDITATION

"These truths have been embedded in the Word of God but are not always apparent to the casual observer" (*The Ancient Portals of Heaven*, p. 14). Have you been able to find the ancient truths and use them to bring God's glory?

_____

_____

_____

_____

_____

_____

_____

_____

DAY 19

I am the door. If anyone enters by Me,
he will be saved, and will go in and
out and find pasture (John 10:9).

DEVOTION FOR TODAY

Jesus is the pathway to enter back into the ancient ways and tap into what the ancients knew and more. Since Abraham, God has chosen the Jewish people to steward the keys and oracles of the Word of God, and from them would come the Jewish Messiah, Savior of the world. God showed the Jewish prophets, apostles, and patriarchs keys and patterns that open up the heavens on the earth. When we connect to these ancient pathways and patterns, we too will see the glory of God unleashed in ways that may have never occurred before. That is why it says, "Salvation is of the Jews" (John 4:22). The 12 Jewish apostles became carriers of the glory that has spread to the entire known world today.

SOMETHING TO THINK ABOUT

1. Why do you think Jesus is the pathway to enter back into the ancient ways and tap into what the ancients knew?

_____

_____

_____

2. What are some keys and patterns that you know God showed some of the Old Testament prophets?

_____

_____

_____

3. How did the apostles tap into the ancient pathways through Jesus? What happened as a result?

_____

_____

_____

MEDITATION

"Jesus is the doorway into knowing God, Heaven, and all that is pure. Any other way, though it may have some power, leads to spiritual death" (*The Ancient Portals of Heaven*, pp. 25–25). How does this truth impact your search for the supernatural?

_____

_____

_____

_____

_____

_____

_____

DAY 20

*Solomon's wisdom excelled the wisdom of all
the people of the East and all the wisdom
of Egypt. For he was wiser than all other
men…* (1 Kings 4:30-31 AMP).

DEVOTION FOR TODAY

Can you imagine that Solomon was wiser than all men on the earth? Besides being the most powerful king in the world, he was a builder, an inventor, an author, a songwriter, and a naturalist who studied all forms of plants, flora, and the entire animal kingdom (see 1 Kings 4:33). All this began simply by Solomon giving a sacrificial offering to God and God asking Solomon what he wanted from Him. Ask God to make you one of His wise men or women and to restore the ancient wisdom He has released on the earth. A good starting place for acquiring this wisdom is to ask God with a humble heart for the fear of the Lord and respect for His ancient people.

SOMETHING TO THINK ABOUT

1. If God asked you what you wanted from Him, would you have selected wisdom as Solomon did? Why or why not?

_____

_____

_____

2. How does the fact that God gave Solomon much more than wisdom affect your sense of priority? Why do you think God blessed Solomon in so many ways?

_____

_____

_____

3. How do humility and respect enter into our search for wisdom and knowledge? How is the fear of the Lord a good starting place for such a quest?

_____

_____

_____

MEDITATION

"During Solomon's time, the ancients knew far more than man did during 'The Dark Ages,' when superstition, ignorance and anti-Semitism reigned" (*The Ancient Portals of Heaven*, p. 51). How does today's world reflect these same negative attributes and ignore the ancient pathways?

_____

_____

_____

_____

_____

_____

_____

_____

DAY 21

A REVIVAL OF WISDOM

The eyes of your understanding being enlightened;
that you may know…what are the riches of the glory
of His inheritance in the saints (Ephesians 1:18).

DEVOTION FOR TODAY

We know that in Heaven there is no lack. Because the Lord told us to pray, "Your will be done on earth as it is in Heaven," we know that God can bring heavenly things to us here on earth. (See Matthew 6:10.) When Heaven's glory comes to earth, you can tap into your inheritance. Once you have a revelation that there is more than enough reserved for you in Heaven, you will no longer walk in lack. As long as you stay in the glory, the treasures of Heaven will be manifested upon the earth. Just as healing, creative miracles, signs, and wonders have been falling from Heaven as a result of the glory, so other heavenly things can come to us.

SOMETHING TO THINK ABOUT

1. Are you truly able to believe that in Heaven there is no lack? Is it easy for you to understand your inheritance that is set aside for you in Heaven? Why or why not?

_____

_____

_____

2. When Jesus prayed for God's will to be done on earth as it is in Heaven, how can we position ourselves to receive His will in all things, even financial things?

_____

_____

_____

3. How do we "stay in the glory"? What makes the glory remain in and around us? What is the result if we stay in God's glory?

_____

_____

_____

MEDITATION

"If we lay up treasure in Heaven, we can make withdrawals from it whenever we get into the glory" (*The Ancient Portals of Heaven*, p. 60). Why is the storehouse in Heaven a better source of supply than laying up treasures on earth?

_____

_____

_____

_____

_____

_____

_____

_____

DAY 22

*You will be brought before governors and
kings for My sake, as a testimony to them
and to the Gentiles* (Matthew 10:18).

DEVOTION FOR TODAY

God is still extending His favor to the Church.
Whether your country is favorable to Christianity or indifferent, or if persecution has
begun, the same glory applies. There have been seasons in which the Church has prospered and grown
in favor with God and man, and there have been
times of great persecution. Supernatural wisdom to
speak to kings is not limited to ideal situations. The
rulers of the world are subject to the glory of God
when it manifests on the earth through you—whatever the situation. God is looking for those He can
use to speak to kings, for they wait to hear the Word
of the Lord. The preaching of the Kingdom of
Heaven is one of the greatest last-day revelations.

SOMETHING TO THINK ABOUT

1. Have you had firsthand experience to see how God is extending favor to the Church? In what ways has He shown His favor to you?

_____

_____

_____

2. Why doesn't it matter whether a country is favorable to Christianity or not in terms of whether God's favor rests with us?

_____

_____

_____

3. Do you think rulers are waiting to hear the word of the Lord? Why or why not? What must we do to be prepared to speak the word of God to them?

_____

_____

_____

MEDITATION

"The wisdom and knowledge of God is being revealed to us so we can walk in the fullness of what has been reserved for us from the beginning" (*The Ancient Portals of Heaven*, p. 90). How can this statement apply to your life today?

_____

_____

_____

_____

_____

_____

_____

Day 23

...ten men...shall grasp the sleeve of a Jewish man, saying, "Let us go with you, for we have heard that God is with you" (Zechariah 8:23).

Devotion for Today

There are ancient geographical locations on the earth today where the gateway or portal to Heaven was once opened in ancient times and still is open to those who access those gateways. These open portals allow greater access into the supernatural, making it easier to access Heaven, revelation, and heavenly encounters. We can access a highway of the supernatural that ancient men of God paved for us through their encounters with God in those very places. We speak much about redigging the wells of revival in places in the Western world that once had a revival. How about revisiting some of the deepest ancient wells that are still open today in Israel—and then taking that glory back to our cities and nations?

SOMETHING TO THINK ABOUT

1. What are some of the possible ancient geographical locations where there has been a gateway opened to Heaven? What did people experience at these locations?

_____

_____

_____

2. Why do you think these gateways might be still open to us today? If we go to these ancient locations, should we expect something supernatural to occur? Why or why not?

_____

_____

_____

3. If we experience the supernatural at an ancient well, how can we "take that glory back" to our cities and nations?

_____

_____

_____

MEDITATION

"The Kingdom of God is around us and with us at all times, but there are also ladders and grids from Heaven to earth that have been set up" (*The Ancient Portals of Heaven*, p. 93). What does this statement mean to you personally?

_____

_____

_____

_____

_____

_____

_____

_____

DAY 24

...shall go up from year to year to worship the King, the Lord of hosts, and to keep the Feast of Tabernacles (Zechariah 14:16).

DEVOTION FOR TODAY

There are times and seasons when the heavens are more open if we access them. The Bible identifies these seasonal open-Heaven grids and even tells us when they are. God promises to visit His people in an unusual way during these special times that He has already marked on His calendar. These are open invitations from God for a holy rendezvous with Him. The feasts are not so much rules to attain any sense of holiness as they are God's perspective and revelation from Heaven so that things on earth may be aligned with what goes on in Heaven. God promised to visit His people during specific seasons of time known as feasts. Why would He not show up during these times today?

SOMETHING TO THINK ABOUT

1. Why do you think that there are times and seasons when the heavens are more easily accessed? What are some of the special feasts and times you know about from Scripture?

   _____

   _____

   _____

2. Is it amazing to think of God having a calendar that revolves around invitations for us to meet with Him? What do you think His purpose is in making such a commitment to us?

   _____

   _____

   _____

3. Do you believe that the ancient feasts are a gateway for us today? How must we protect the opportunity and not make it into a dead ritual?

   _____

   _____

   _____

MEDITATION

"God opened the heavens in both the Old and New Testament during these seasons" (*The Ancient Portals of Heaven*, p. 116). What did God do during the Feast of Pentecost in the Old Testament? What did He do during the same Feast in the New Testament? What might He do today?

_____

_____

_____

_____

_____

_____

_____

DAY 25

...give to you the spirit of wisdom and revelation...the exceeding greatness of His power... (Ephesians 1:17-19).

DEVOTION FOR TODAY

As it was in the days of Elijah, Elisha, and Jesus, so today a new release of resurrections will be seen. Jesus commanded His disciples to raise the dead, heal the sick, and cleanse the leper—all in the same command form. The Lord will not only release His power to us, but He will also release revelation in order to know the workings of His power. It's no use having power without the knowledge about how to use it. I believe that God is revealing revelation knowledge so believers will know not just the power but also how the power works— even for raising the dead. The spirit of Elijah will once again be fully resurrected in our day.

SOMETHING TO THINK ABOUT

1. Does the idea of God using you to raise the dead seem foreign to you? Why or why not?

_____

_____

_____

2. Why is revelation knowledge so important for us as God releases His power to us in these days?

_____

_____

_____

3. How do we tap into the revelation knowledge so we can be ready to do the acts of power God wants us to do?

_____

_____

_____

MEDITATION

"God is restoring everything in these days and will do so with even greater power" (*The Ancient Portals of Heaven*, p. 132). Why do you believe God desires to use us to demonstrate even greater power than Elijah, Elisha, or even Jesus?

_____

_____

_____

_____

_____

_____

_____

_____

DAY 26

Prophesy to the breath…"Come … O breath, and breathe on these slain, that they may live." So I prophesied…and breath came into them… (Ezekiel 37:9-10).

DEVOTION FOR TODAY

Life was breathed into the man's nostrils by God (see Gen. 2:7). God symbolically put His face to Adam's face and brought life to him. What God did was breathe "spirit" into man. A person with only a body but no human spirit has no life. Life is in the spirit of a person. When someone dies, the spirit of the person departs from the body. If the human spirit returns to the body, life returns. The word *breath* in God's command to the prophet is really translated as "spirit" when translated literally from the original Hebrew. The spirit of a man or woman returning to their body is the key to raising the dead.

107

SOMETHING TO THINK ABOUT

1. Describe what your spirit is inside of you. How does the fact that God breathed the spirit into mankind separate us from other creatures?

_____

_____

_____

2. When a person dies, what happens to his or her spirit? How does a person's spirit define if he or she is alive or dead?

_____

_____

_____

3. If the key to raising the dead is having a person's spirit return to him or her, how does this fact guide our prayers to greater effectiveness?

_____

_____

_____

MEDITATION

"Don't ever forget that a new revelation brings a new manifestation of God" (*The Ancient Portals of Heaven,* p. 136). How can you apply this truth to your life in order to see an increase in the manifestations of God's power?

_____

_____

_____

_____

_____

_____

_____

_____

DAY 27

NOT DEAD, ONLY SLEEPING

*...and after that He said to them,
"Our friend Lazarus sleeps, but I go
that I may wake him up"* (John 11:11).

DEVOTION FOR TODAY

How could Jesus say that Lazarus was not dead when clearly, by all human measures, he was as dead as any other corpse? Because Lazarus knew Jesus. After the life of Jesus touches a life and breathes on it, it can never die. Because you have a living, personal relationship with the Messiah, you will never die. Anything that God has breathed on receives life; it may seem dead, but it is only sleeping. Because Lazarus' life was totally devoted to God's Kingdom, Jesus could easily pull him from Heaven to earth. When God has touched something in your life, it never dies, even if it seems like it is not moving. It is not lost because He has already touched it.

SOMETHING TO THINK ABOUT

1. Has God spoken or prophesied some things over your life that once had life and now seem dead? What should you believe about those things?

_____

_____

_____

2. Did God use you powerfully in a certain way and now it seems to be lost or gone? Do you believe that the potential is just sleeping?

_____

_____

_____

3. Did God heal you and you seem to have lost that healing? Do you have the faith to believe that the healing is not dead?

_____

_____

_____

MEDITATION

"Maybe you have unfulfilled promises. If they were God-breathed, then they are not dead" (*The Ancient Portals of Heaven,* p. 138). Meditate on the promises God has spoken to your heart about you personally. What should you believe about these unfulfilled promises?

_____

_____

_____

_____

_____

_____

_____

DAY 28

RESURRECTION GLORY AND ISRAEL

…I will send you Elijah…he will turn the hearts of the fathers to the children, and the hearts of the children to their fathers… (Malachi 4:5-6).

DEVOTION FOR TODAY

The early Church walked on a level of resurrection glory and power that we have yet to see. What was their secret? How did they tap into this extreme glory? Malachi 4 talks about the spirit of Elijah being restored in the last days. The return of the spirit of Elijah is connected to the hearts of fathers turning to their children and the children to their fathers. The Jewish people are the spiritual fathers of the faith. The Gentile Church today is the children and offspring of the Jewish apostles and prophets. We have been disconnected from each other for over 2,000 years. As we are reconnected to each other, the resurrection power of God that the early Church walked in will be unlocked.

SOMETHING TO THINK ABOUT

1. What do you think the early Church's secret was for walking in resurrection glory and power? Is the secret the same for the Church today?

_____

_____

_____

2. Why do you think the resurrection glory and power is tied into relationships (Mal. 4)?

_____

_____

_____

3. In your opinion, why is the Gentile Church still disconnected with the Jewish people? What is the result of this disconnect?

_____

_____

_____

MEDITATION

"God is about to unleash a wave of resurrection glory to ministries and churches that will reconnect to the root and help Israel return to her Messiah" (*The Ancient Portals of Heaven,* p. 142). Think about ways in which you might help this happen.

_____

_____

_____

_____

_____

_____

_____

_____

DAY 29

ELISHA'S DOUBLE PORTION

*…Elijah said to Elisha, "…What may I do for
you …" Elisha said, "…let a double portion
of your spirit be upon me"* (2 Kings 2:9).

DEVOTION FOR TODAY

Elisha wanted to be just like his spiritual father, Elijah. That is the reason he asked for a double portion. Elisha wanted to continue the legacy so Elijah, in a sense, would live on through the same glory, yet stronger. It is recorded that Elijah performed seven major miracles—Elisha is credited with fourteen. The *"Elisha glory"* is when the torch of the last generation is passed to the next generation with even greater power. To operate in this realm, there are some important principles to understand. Recently, several spiritual leaders and apostles of the faith have gone on to be with the Lord—now is the time to walk into the Elisha mantle and continue where they left off.

SOMETHING TO THINK ABOUT

1. Just as Elisha wanted to be like his spiritual father, Elijah, is there someone that you see as a spiritual mother or father in your life?

   _____

   _____

   _____

2. How is it possible that the glory of one person could live on in another? What legacy of God's glory are you leaving in someone else?

   _____

   _____

   _____

3. How are torches passed from one generation to another? Are you in line with someone from an older generation to receive a torch?

   _____

   _____

   _____

MEDITATION

"Elisha's bones so held the glory that when a dead man was thrown onto Elisha's bones in the same grave, the man was instantly resurrected!" (see 2 Kings 13:21) (*The Ancient Portals of Heaven,* p. 155). What would happen if this took place today?

_____

_____

_____

_____

_____

_____

_____

_____

Day 30

The Master Key to the Double Portion

Many of the people of Israel are now enemies of the Good News, and this benefits you Gentiles. Yet they are still the people He loves... (Romans 11:28-29 NLT).

Devotion for Today

Each generation that honored its fathers received an even greater blessing. Abraham left a spiritual inheritance to his son Isaac. Isaac was born already with a blessed status, and whatever else he would do for God would add to and double that blessing. If we cut ourselves off from identifying with the Jewish people, we lose that generational blessing and are cut off from the root of where the blessings began. The blessings came out of Abraham and the Jewish people. As we recognize how we have been grafted in, and become "a partaker of the root and fatness of the olive tree," we tap into all the blessings from the time of Abraham through to Jesus, the early church, and today (see Rom. 11:17).

SOMETHING TO THINK ABOUT

1. Why do you think God set up the principle of honoring fathers and receiving a greater blessing?

_____

_____

_____

2. Who has given spiritual blessings to you, whether it be a biological family member or a spiritual family member? What blessings have you received?

_____

_____

_____

3. How are you adding to the blessing you have and doubling it for the generation to come? What are you adding?

_____

_____

_____

MEDITATION

"Take a strong stand with your forefather Israel and see the inheritance and double portion come upon you" (*The Ancient Portals of Heaven,* p. 163). How can you make this stand? How does intercession play a part in your stand?

_____

_____

_____

_____

_____

_____

_____

DAY 31

*…I magnify my ministry, if…I may
provoke to jealousy those who are my flesh
and save some…* (Romans 11:13-14).

DEVOTION FOR TODAY

In Romans 11, Paul explains to Gentile believers
in Rome the master key to the success of his life
and ministry. His secret is that he would always
go to the Jews first with the Gospel, make them jealous for the Messiah, and try to save some. Why would
this be the master key to world harvest then or today?
Although Paul was called by God to take the Gospel
to the Gentiles, his initial desire was to be called to
the Jews. But God had other plans. Paul had a key
that would win Gentiles. He knew the Hebrew writ-
ings that said, *"I will bless those who bless you* [Israel],
and I will curse him who curses you" (Gen. 12:3).

SOMETHING TO THINK ABOUT

1. How did Paul know that the master key to the success of his ministry was to reach the Jews first—especially when he was called to the Gentiles?

   _____

   _____

   _____

2. Why do you think the Jewish people are not jealous for the Messiah at this point in time when looking at Christians? What would make them jealous?

   _____

   _____

   _____

3. How does the covenant God made with Abraham affect the blessings that you receive today?

   _____

   _____

   _____

MEDITATION

"There are ancient keys that will unlock and accelerate worldwide harvest more than anything else on the planet; they are seldom used but are now being revealed once again" (*The Ancient Portals of Heaven,* p. 171). Why is honoring Israel the master key?

_____

_____

_____

_____

_____

_____

_____

_____

DAY 32

THE GENTILE KEY

…to provoke them to jealousy, salvation has come to the Gentiles (Romans 11:11).

DEVOTION FOR TODAY

In Romans 10:1-2, Paul says, *"My heart's desire and prayer to God for Israel is that they may be saved."* He says that God wouldn't let him reach Israel as his main and only call. Every believer in Jesus has a calling to the Jewish people in Israel and around the world, to make them jealous by your salvation, love, healing, signs and wonders, family, blessings, and so on. Reaching Israel accelerates salvation worldwide among Gentiles, and reaching those Gentiles with salvation who will love Israel also speeds up Israel's revival. As you go to the nations to bring in the harvest, do it with a goal that these Gentiles will cause Israel to be saved.

SOMETHING TO THINK ABOUT

1. Does it seem to you a round-about way to reach Israel by reaching Gentiles first? Why or why not?

   _____

   _____

   _____

2. How does reaching Israel accelerate salvation among Gentiles? How does reaching Gentiles reciprocate salvation to Israel?

   _____

   _____

   _____

3. Have you been making any Jewish people jealous lately? What do you need to do in order to make Jews jealous of your Messiah?

   _____

   _____

   _____

MEDITATION

"Who better to provoke Israel to jealousy than the descendents of Ishmael?" (*The Ancient Portals of Heaven,* p. 186). Think about the initial break in relationship between Isaac and Ishmael and the historical rift between their descendents to answer the question.

_____

_____

_____

_____

_____

_____

_____

DAY 33

THE ISHMAEL-MUSLIM CONNECTION

*…I will provoke you to jealousy by those who
are not a nation, I will move you to anger
by a foolish nation* (Romans 10:19).

DEVOTION FOR TODAY

Romans 11:25 says that *"…blindness in part
has happened to Israel until the fullness of the
Gentiles has come in."* According to Faisal
Malick (a former Muslim, now a believer) in his
book *Here Comes Ishmael,* nearly 42 percent of the
world's Gentile population is Muslim.[1] That means
that as we start to reach the last remnant of the Gentile world, the Muslims, more Jews in Israel and
worldwide will be saved as the veil gets lifted more
and more. As you accept the call to take the Gospel
to the Muslims, you will also be part of lifting the veil
off the Jews, and as you bless the Jews and reach
them with salvation, it will trigger greater harvests
among the Gentiles.

SOMETHING TO THINK ABOUT

1. What is the "blindness" that is over Israel? Why would God want to keep Israel blinded to the truth for the sake of reaching Gentiles?

   _____

   _____

   _____

2. How well are you acquainted with the demographics of the Muslim world population? Do you think this knowledge would be helpful in your prayers for them?

   _____

   _____

   _____

3. Do you personally know Muslims? Do you have opportunities to reach into their community and let your life be a witness of God's grace?

   _____

   _____

   _____

MEDITATION

"The Muslim harvest will also trigger a harvest of souls in many other nations especially in Israel" (*The Ancient Portals of Heaven,* p. 186). Why is this true? How will world evangelism get a boost if Muslims are reached for the Gospel of Jesus Christ?

_____

_____

_____

_____

_____

_____

_____

_____

ENDNOTE

1. Faisal Malick, *Here Comes Ishmael: The Kairos Moment for the Muslim People* (Bellville, Ontario: Essence Publishing, 2005).

DAY 34

THE RISE AND FALL OF NATIONS

I will make your name great...I will
bless those who bless you, and I will curse
him who curses you (Genesis 12:2-3).

DEVOTION FOR TODAY

There are ancient mysteries that will cause a nation to rise or to fall based on the wisdom and knowledge of the ancients embedded in the Word of God. America, for example, has seen significant blessing and has risen as the most blessed nation on the earth by following these time-tested, ancient blessings. Every world empire that had the most Jews within its borders or the most direct influence with the Jewish people were also among the most powerful nations on the earth, and those same nations fell based on what they did to the Jewish people. God sets before us two paths, blessings or curses. Let's choose the blessing of God, aligning our lives with God's purposes for His covenant people, land, and nation.

SOMETHING TO THINK ABOUT

1. Why do you think God has blessed nations who have blessed the Jews and cursed nations who have cursed the Jewish people?

   _____

   _____

   _____

2. In the world's perspective of "fairness," why does blessing Israel seem to play favorites with the Jews and disrespect the nations around them, and how has this subtle anti-Semitic train of thought led to such hatred?

   _____

   _____

   _____

3. How might you help influence people who represent you in the government to bless Israel?

   _____

   _____

   _____

MEDITATION

"As you begin to bless, stand with, and pray for revival and harvest in Israel, a new wave of favor, glory, and blessing of God will begin to invade your life" (*The Ancient Portals of Heaven,* p. 216). Have you determined to do this?

_____

_____

_____

_____

_____

_____

_____

_____

Day 35

The Glory Zone

*…the worlds were framed by the Word of God,
so that the things which are seen were not made
of things which are visible* (Hebrews 11:3).

Devotion for Today

It says in Scripture that everything that was made was made of things that are not visible. Genesis 1:1-2 tells us that the first invisible thing God sent was His own Spirit or Glory upon the earth. The first ingredient is the Glory. Once you are in a *glory zone,* anything is possible. God used His own Spirit as the first major ingredient. The second invisible ingredient is sound: *"And God said…"* (Gen. 1:3). Only God's voice could have created everything, since nothing was created before this. God spoke and everything was created. After the atmosphere of the glory and presence of God was on the earth, all God had to do was speak into His own cloud of His glory.

SOMETHING TO THINK ABOUT

1. God did not create the world out of nothing but out of things that are invisible. How do you know that this is true?

   _____

   _____

   _____

2. Why do you think God sent His Glory or Spirit as the first invisible ingredient of creation? How does God's Glory or Spirit work in us today?

   _____

   _____

   _____

3. Why do you think sound is the second ingredient God used in creation? How does the spoken Word of God work today?

   _____

   _____

   _____

MEDITATION

"When you are in the *glory zone* and speak out what God is telling or showing you, things will start to be created at that moment" (*Glory Invasion,* p. 23). Have you had any experience in the glory zone?

_____

_____

_____

_____

_____

_____

_____

_____

Day 36

The Ingredient of Sound

*Praise Him, sun and moon; Praise Him, all
you stars of light…Praise the Lord from the
earth…Mountains and all hills…* (Psalm 148:3,9).

Devotion for Today

In Psalm 148 God commands the sun, moon, and stars to praise Him. He even commands mountains and hills to praise Him. Only an intelligent God who knows His creation intimately can command seemingly inanimate objects to respond in worship to Him. In fact, all creation has the ability to hear, listen, obey, respond, and worship its Creator. Often when you are outdoors, you sense His presence because there is a natural, ongoing orchestra of worship via the creation that welcomes the presence of God. All of His creation not only hears and understands but also replies and worships Him. This being true, the creation also can respond to you when you speak words of faith directed by God in the glory realm.

SOMETHING TO THINK ABOUT

1. How is it possible for inanimate objects of creation to worship God, the Creator? In what ways do they worship?

_____

_____

_____

2. Have you sensed God's presence in the beauty of nature? Explain the feelings that you have had and how you knew God was near.

_____

_____

_____

3. How can creation respond to us when we speak words of faith in the glory realm? How do you know that creation has the capacity to respond to you?

_____

_____

_____

Meditation

"Jesus said we could speak to a mountain and it is possible for it to be removed (see Matthew 17:20). This realization opens a new world of authority over creation" (*Glory Invasion*, p. 29). How does this open your world?

_____

_____

_____

_____

_____

_____

_____

_____

DAY 37

CREATIVE MIRACLES

*For everyone who asks receives, and he
who seeks finds, and to him who knocks
it will be opened* (Luke 11:10).

DEVOTION FOR TODAY

If we only see God as the Healer and focus our
preaching and receiving on healing, then we will
only see healings but not *creative miracles*. In
order to see the creative we must see God as Creator.
We must know God more as the Creator than as the
Healer in order to abound in the creative miracles.
The reason: God manifests the way you perceive
Him. For example, some churches focus on the God
of salvation and consequently they witness many salvations, but not healings. Other churches emphasize
a God who delivers, and He manifests as such. God
will manifest in the way you perceive Him. Do not
limit God—see Him in unlimited aspects and you
will see unlimited manifestations of Him.

SOMETHING TO THINK ABOUT

1. What is the difference between a healing and a creative miracle? Why do you think our focus must be different in order to see creative miracles in our midst?

   _____

   _____

   _____

2. What aspects of God do we need to understand and experience if we are to know God as Creator?

   _____

   _____

   _____

3. How do our perceptions of God dictate the ways in which God will manifest Himself? How can this be limiting to our experience of His presence?

   _____

   _____

   _____

MEDITATION

"When you are experiencing extreme glory you are, in essence, in an expanded glory" (*Glory Invasion,* p. 48). Think about how Jesus' resurrected body demonstrated this to the disciples. Can you imagine doing the same kinds of things Jesus did?

_____

_____

_____

_____

_____

_____

_____

DAY 38

*For you were called to freedom, brethren…If
we live by the Spirit, let us also walk by
the Spirit* (Galatians 5:13,25 NASB).

DEVOTION FOR TODAY

By faith, Peter asked to join Jesus as He walked on the water. Peter lunged into the glory realm where his body weight did not make him sink but the water actually became solid enough for him to walk on. He was supported by the knowledge of his spirit and not his intellect. Walk by the spirit, not the flesh. The flesh is your natural, three-dimensional, limited way of thinking. As soon as Peter began to analyze and revert to past experience, he began to sink. He did not understand how he was walking on water. He simply did by faith. Faith with action combined with the glory will get you into the realm of creative miracles faster than anything else—even if you don't understand it.

SOMETHING TO THINK ABOUT

1. What is the difference between the knowledge of your spirit and the knowledge of your intellect?

   _____

   _____

   _____

2. What are the marks of someone who walks by the spirit? What the marks of someone who walks by the flesh?

   _____

   _____

   _____

3. How do faith and action combine to get us into the glory realm faster than anything else?

   _____

   _____

   _____

MEDITATION

"Peter defied the three-dimensional law of the world and operated out of Heaven's fourth or unlimited dimension" (*Glory Invasion,* p. 50). Think about the possibilities that could come to you when you operate out of Heaven's unlimited dimension.

_____

_____

_____

_____

_____

_____

_____

DAY 39

REVELATORY REALMS AND PORTALS

I, John, both your brother and companion…I was in the Spirit on the Lord's Day, and I heard behind me a loud voice… (Revelation 1:9-10).

DEVOTION FOR TODAY

Visitations, dreams, visions, and heavenly experiences are of great worth. They can alter and accelerate years of your life and ministry because of one heavenly encounter. Mary was changed with one angelic visit, as were Moses, Joshua, Joseph, David, Elizabeth, and many more. Just as you can be transported over the earth because of the glory, you can also be transported upward to Heaven. Your spirit, and at times your spirit and body, can be taken there. The apostle Paul could not tell if his spirit only or both his body and spirit were taken to Heaven to see things, many of which he was not allowed to describe. In the *glory zone* there is no distance between time and space, Heaven or earth.

159

SOMETHING TO THINK ABOUT

1. What is the significance behind dreams, visions, and heavenly experiences? How can these encounters change a life?

_____

_____

_____

2. When someone is transported to Heaven and back, does he or she need to die and come back to life? Think of some examples to support your answer.

_____

_____

_____

3. How can there be no distance between time and space, Heaven and earth in the glory zone? How does this work?

_____

_____

_____

MEDITATION

"There are many testimonies of God's modern-day believers that refer to revelatory realms and heavenly portals" (*Glory Invasion,* p. 59). Have you experienced revelatory realms or heavenly portals? What puts someone in the position of receiving such experiences?

_____

_____

_____

_____

_____

_____

_____

DAY 40

PROPHETIC GLORY

Having then gifts differing according to the grace that is given to us, let us use them: if prophecy, let us prophesy in proportion to our faith (Romans 12:6).

DEVOTION FOR TODAY

You can have a prophetic gifting flow at times even when you are not necessarily in the glory. God's gifts are irrevocable but not always operated in the glory realm.

The same goes for those with a healing anointing. Just because there are healings, prophecies, or gifts in operation does not mean that the glory of God is present. Some will say, *"Lord, Lord have we not prophesied in your name?"* The Lord's response is, *"I never knew you"* (Matt. 7:22-23). If you first put the primary emphasis on the glory, which only comes through intimacy with Him, a close relationship, and times of waiting on the Lord, then when you do prophesy the prophecy will be earth shaking and change entire nations.

SOMETHING TO THINK ABOUT

1. How can someone have a prophetic or healing gifting flow at times that person is not necessarily in the glory?

_____

_____

_____

2. How can we know whether God is present as the prophetic or healing gift flow in meetings? What are the marks of a glory zone?

_____

_____

_____

3. What should be the primary emphasis for everyone who operates in any supernatural gifting? Why is this so important?

_____

_____

_____

MEDITATION

"We can't use the gift without the Giver. That is why I call it *prophetic glory!*" (*Glory Invasion,* p. 72). Think about this statement in the light of your experience. In what ways are the Giver and the gift intertwined?

_____

_____

_____

_____

_____

_____

_____

_____

DAY 41

GREATER GLORY

I am the vine…He who abides in Me, and
I in him, bears much fruit; for without
Me you can do nothing (John 15:5).

DEVOTION FOR TODAY

The greater the glory, the quicker things will happen. After a glory-filled prophecy is given, the only thing to do is believe it. That is very important and should not be neglected. The greater the glory the greater the miracles, but also the greater the judgment—swift miracles, but also swift correction or judgment. Both are accelerated as the glory is accelerated, depending on our response. When the glory is present, there is great power in our words. Often, our words are prophetic, whether we realize it or not. That which we speak while in the glory is very important.

The next time the glory comes in a meeting, be careful of careless words or of creating something with words that God did not intend.

167

SOMETHING TO THINK ABOUT

1. Define what a "glory-filled" prophecy is. How does it demonstrate its power from other prophetic utterances?

   _____

   _____

   _____

2. Why do you think speed is associated with greater glory? Why would God want to demonstrate the supernatural so quickly?

   _____

   _____

   _____

3. Why do you think the greater glory creates greater miracles? Why does it also bring greater judgment?

   _____

   _____

   _____

MEDITATION

"When the glory goes to a greater level, so does the prophetic gift and the swiftness of it" (*Glory Invasion,* p. 78). How can you distinguish a greater level of glory as it comes to a meeting or worship service?

_____

_____

_____

_____

_____

_____

_____

Day 42

Reaping Glory

*May the Lord, the God of your fathers, increase
you a thousand-fold more than you are and bless you, just
as He has promised you!* (Deuteronomy 1:11 NASB)

Devotion for Today

In the Old and New Testaments, whenever the glory of God appeared, Israel stopped and took up an offering to honor the God of glory. It was an automatic response to the glory that God required when manifest presence and glory appeared—not because He needs it but because He knows that this is what man treasures the most—his gold and silver and provision. It is one of the highest acts of worship to give up something for God's glory that is truly, personally costly. When the glory comes or God tells you to sow into a ministry or place where the glory is moving, giving generously into that which God is already blessing with His glory will cause the greatest return.

SOMETHING TO THINK ABOUT

1. How are offerings tied to an appearance of the glory of God in the Scriptures? Do we tend to see the same connection today? Why or why not?

_____

_____

_____

2. Why does giving God the treasures of man's heart (gold, money) please God? What do these gifts signify from man's heart to God's heart?

_____

_____

_____

3. What does "sow generously" mean? What kind of sliding scale is a "generous" gift? Why is being generous so important?

_____

_____

_____

MEDITATION

"It is not selfish if your motives for receiving are good and for His glory" (*Glory Invasion,* p. 90). Have you been selfish when you asked for material blessings from God? When you sow, do you expect to reap as any farmer does?

_____

_____

_____

_____

_____

_____

_____

_____

DAY 43

REAPING WHERE YOU DID NOT SOW

I have given you a land for which you did not labor, and cities which you did not build…you eat…which you did not plant (Joshua 24:13).

DEVOTION FOR TODAY

After you have been faithful to sow sacrificially and then purposely reap what you sowed, you can enter the next dimension of *reaping where you did not sow*. This is the realm of living in the over and above, where you go to where your cup is running over. Few enter this realm because they don't master the sacrificial sowing or the violent reaping dimension on a consistent basis. The key is to declare with your mouth, "I reap where I have never sowed." After you declare it out loud, angels are released to "hearken to the Word of God." They react as if God Himself is declaring it. That is the authority that comes when you declare a revelation from Heaven.

SOMETHING TO THINK ABOUT

1. What are the two prerequisites for reaping where you did not sow? Why do you think these two disciplines are important before entering into this realm?

   _____

   _____

   _____

2. Why do you think it is important to declare that you will reap where you have never sown with your mouth?

   _____

   _____

   _____

3. Have you considered before the authority you have to command angels when you speak the Word of God as a revelation from Heaven?

   _____

   _____

   _____

Meditation

"The purpose and motive for entering this realm must simply be to be a blessing to others. We must purge ourselves of all selfish desires" (*Glory Invasion*, p. 99). What must you do to purge yourself of greed and selfishness, and why does giving help you to be set free of these things?

_____

_____

_____

_____

_____

_____

_____

DAY 44

*Nations will come to your light, and kings
to the brightness of your rising… They all gather
together, they come to you…* (Isaiah 60:3-4).

DEVOTION FOR TODAY

The Church has often been satisfied with the prophetic gifts staying confined within their churches, home groups, or special conferences, blessing only each other with words. But these are only the starting places where there is room to learn and grow in these gifts. Now is the time for God to showcase His prophetic glory to the heads of nations so they will be confronted with God's Word and power. God greatly desires to speak to world leaders and those in positions of influence such as actors, athletes, bankers, and business men and women—people desperately looking for an answer to major worldwide crises. There must be enough vessels prepared, trained, trustworthy, and purified to carry out this task.

179

SOMETHING TO THINK ABOUT

1. Why should the prophetic gifts be used outside the Church as well as inside its walls? What are some prophets in the Old Testament that prophesied to rulers?

   _____

   _____

   _____

2. What reaction do you think the prophetic glory will have among those in authority and influence in the nations?

   _____

   _____

   _____

3. What must we do to prepare to be used to bring the prophetic glory to people who are in positions of influence?

   _____

   _____

   _____

MEDITATION

"A man's gift makes room for him and brings him before great men" (Prov. 18:16). What does this verse mean to you personally? What great men does God want you to meet?

_____

_____

_____

_____

_____

_____

_____

_____

DAY 45

*Arise, shine; ...the Glory of the Lord
is risen upon you....And His Glory* [light]
will be seen upon you (Isaiah 60:1-2).

DEVOTION FOR TODAY

If you had a tumor and walked into Heaven, how long do you think it would take you to be healed? How long would it take you to get deliverance in Heaven? Instantly, right? The reason: the glory that is in Heaven. In the glory there is no sickness or demons because just as in Heaven, they are not allowed to enter. If God's will is to be done *on the earth as it is in Heaven*, then the one ingredient missing from earth as it is in Heaven is the *glory*. When that glory appears on the earth, then we can say and expect with confidence that His will be done as rapidly on the earth as it would be in Heaven.

SOMETHING TO THINK ABOUT

1. Why is there no sickness or demons in Heaven? What does the glory do to eliminate these?

   _____

   _____

   _____

2. How is it possible for God's will to be done on earth as it is in Heaven? What does glory have to do with His will?

   _____

   _____

   _____

3. How does the appearance of God's glory give us confidence? How does that glory make a difference as to how quickly His will is manifest on earth?

   _____

   _____

   _____

MEDITATION

"When the Lord Himself appears in His glory or brings His presence, evil flees" (*Glory Invasion,* p. 122). How might practicing the presence of the Lord and being in His glory prepare you for when evil comes your way?

_____

_____

_____

_____

_____

_____

_____

_____

DAY 46

WAIT UNTIL THE SPIRIT MOVES

...open for you the windows of heaven and pour out...such blessing that there will not be room enough to receive it (Malachi 3:10).

DEVOTION FOR TODAY

You may be asking, "How do I get the glory to come?" There are several things that open up the glory realm. *Holiness* is one of them. Pursue holiness so you can keep the channels and intimacy with God open. *Praise and worship* also quickly transport you into an atmosphere of the glory of God. The third way to usher in the glory is *fasting and prayer*. When you fast and pray you are breaking through into the glory realm at an accelerated pace. When you fast, you are telling God that His glory is more important to you than even food. Another key to ushering in the glory is *sacrificial giving*. It opens up the glory and miracles in ways that nothing else will.

SOMETHING TO THINK ABOUT

1. How do you "pursue holiness"? What makes someone holy? Are we ever able to attain holiness on earth?

2. Have you experienced the glory realm during a period of prayer and fasting? How does priority come into play in this case?

3. When you sacrifice to give, how does this open the way for the glory? How do you know the difference between giving and giving sacrificially?

MEDITATION

"Basically you should praise until the spirit of worship comes" (*Glory Invasion,* p. 132). Do you understand the meaning of this statement? Allow yourself to give time on a daily basis to praise God until the spirit of worship comes.

_____

_____

_____

_____

_____

_____

_____

_____

DAY 47

WHEN THE SPIRIT MOVES

*The wind blows…and you hear the
sound…but cannot tell where…where it goes.
So is everyone…born of the Spirit* (John 3:8).

DEVOTION FOR TODAY

It is one thing to get the glory and Spirit of God
to come; it is another thing to get Him to move.
Our sensitivity to His moving needs to be developed. In Genesis, as soon as the Spirit began to move
over the waters, God spoke. We have to wait until the
Spirit moves before we declare things or pray for miracles. Once the Spirit has moved, then you step out
in faith and do or say that which God is doing or saying while He is moving. After the presence of God's
glory has moved, you can be sure that God has
already gone before you to perform what you will say
or do. Now you can pick the fruit.

SOMETHING TO THINK ABOUT

1. What is the difference between getting the Spirit of God to come and getting Him to move?

   _____

   _____

   _____

2. Why do we need to wait for the Spirit to move before we declare prophetically or pray for miracles?

   _____

   _____

   _____

3. To know the presence of God's glory has moved gives us confidence. Why? How do you know that you are able to pick the fruit?

   _____

   _____

   _____

Meditation

"How do you know when the Spirit is moving? It is similar to the wind—you know when the wind is moving even though you can't see it...you can sense it" (*Glory Invasion*, p. 136). Make time to practice this.

_____

_____

_____

_____

_____

_____

_____

DAY 48

And he stretched himself out on the child three times…and the soul of the child came back to him, and he revived (1 Kings 17:21-22).

DEVOTION FOR TODAY

As it was in the days of Elijah, Elisha, and Jesus, we are today going to see a new release of resurrections as never before. The Lord will not only release His power to us which He already has, but it also says He will release revelation in order to know the *workings* of His power. It's no use having power without the knowledge about how to use it. I believe that God is revealing revelation knowledge in these days so believers will know not just the power but also how the power works—even for raising the dead. God is restoring everything in these days and will do so with even greater power. The spirit of Elijah will once again be fully resurrected in our day!

SOMETHING TO THINK ABOUT

1. From what you understand, is resurrection from the dead any more difficult in God's eyes than healing? Why or why not?

_____

_____

_____

2. How does the knowledge of God's power work so that we can see people raised from the dead?

_____

_____

_____

3. What does it mean to you that God is going to restore everything to us, but with greater power?

_____

_____

_____

Meditation

"Life is in the spirit of a person" (*Glory Invasion,* p. 144). What does this statement mean to you? How must a dead body respond if a human spirit returns to the body? What is the breath of God?

_____

_____

_____

_____

_____

_____

_____

_____

DAY 49

ABUNDANT GLORY

*I will put My Spirit in you and you shall
live…Then you shall know that I, the Lord,
have spoken it and performed it…* (Ezekiel 37:14).

DEVOTION FOR TODAY

One revelation from God is all it takes to see a new manifestation of His abundant glory. Don't ever forget that a new revelation brings a new manifestation of God. We need to continually seek God for fresher and clearer revelation into the things of God for a greater and more powerful manifestation of God's glory in the world in these last days. He is just waiting for you to realize the revelation that your dream, prophecy, revelation, desire, or miracle is not dead—only sleeping! He is ready to awaken those promises as you open yourself to His abundant glory. God has manifested His *resurrection glory* in times past in different ways, and today is no different because God never changes.

SOMETHING TO THINK ABOUT

1. Do we have to have every revelation before we can move out in the manifestations of God's glory? Why or why not?

   _____

   _____

   _____

2. How does God give us revelations to match manifestations He is performing? How do we receive these revelations?

   _____

   _____

   _____

3. How does God awaken the dreams, prophecies, revelations, desires, or miracles that are sleeping inside of us?

   _____

   _____

   _____

MEDITATION

"Believers in the Kingdom of God never really die as we are now made alive in Christ whether in the body or Spirit" (*Glory Invasion*, p. 148). Think about what this means to you personally in your life and in your death.

_____

_____

_____

_____

_____

_____

_____

_____

DAY 50

THE ELISHA GLORY

*Because I love Zion, I will not keep still... I
will not stop praying for her until her righteousness
shines like the dawn...* (Isaiah 62:1 NLT).

DEVOTION FOR TODAY

I have noticed something important about those
who walk with some of the greatest mantles—
they also honor Israel and the Jewish people
who are the spiritual parents of all believers and the
Church. Ministries that are sincerely praying, fasting,
and interceding for our spiritual parents, Israel and
the Jews who birthed us into the faith, will experience a whole new dimension in God. We see a generational blessing that doubles and multiplies. If we
cut ourselves off from identifying with the Jewish
people, we lose that generational blessing and are cut
off from the root of where the blessings began. As we
re-plug ourselves into that root, we tap into all the
blessings beginning with Abraham all the way to Jesus,
the early Church, and today.

SOMETHING TO THINK ABOUT

1. How passionate are you about your love for Israel and the Jewish people? Do you understand God's heart for them?

   _____

   _____

   _____

2. Why do you think the ministries that are sincerely praying, fasting, and interceding for the Jewish people have some of the greatest mantles on them?

   _____

   _____

   _____

3. What is your understanding as to how a generational blessing is given? How do we multiply our generational blessings from blessing Israel?

   _____

   _____

   _____

Meditation

"Take a strong stand with your forefather Israel and see the inheritance and double portion come upon you" (*Glory Invasion,* p. 167). How might you "take a strong stand" with Israel? What does this mean to you in a practical sense?

_____

_____

_____

_____

_____

_____

_____

AUTHOR CONTACT INFORMATION

For more information, visit us online at:
www.thegloryzone.org.
Or write to:
David Herzog Ministries
P.O. Box 2070
Sedona, AZ 86339

Additional copies of this book and other
book titles from DESTINY IMAGE are
available at your local bookstore.

Call toll-free: 1-800-722-6774.

Send a request for a catalog to:

Destiny Image® Publishers, Inc.

P.O. Box 310
Shippensburg, PA 17257-0310

*"Speaking to the Purposes of God for This
Generation and for the Generations to Come."*

For a complete list of our titles,
visit us at www.destinyimage.com.